# WHEN MOMMY TUCKS THE STARS IN

By: Erik Usher

This book is dedicated to all the families of those First responders who selflessly spend nights away from their families to help yours.

More importantly, this is for my wonderful wife who had to answer this questions to our two children Maya and Max!

"When Mommy Tucks The Stars In"
Copyright © 2024 by Erik Usher

All rights reserved. No part of this publication may be reproduced or transmitted in any form or by any means, electronic or mechanical, Including photocopying, recording or any information storage and retrieval system, without written permission from the copyright owner.

"Why isn't Mommy home tonight?" asked Maya, hugging her stuffed dalmatian tightly. The soft glow of her bedside lamp lit up the room as she gazed at Daddy with curious eyes.

"Well, Maya," said Dad, tucking her in, "Mommy is out helping people tonight. She's a firefighter, and that means she's always ready to protect people when they're in trouble."

"Is Mommy putting out big fires?" Maya asked, her eyes wide with wonder.

"Sometimes," Dad said with a nod. "But she also helps in so many other ways, like rescuing people or making sure their homes are safe."

"Is it scary for her?" Maya whispered.

"A little," Dad said softly. "But Mommy is very brave. She trains with her team to stay safe and to protect others, no matter how hard the job is."

"Does Mommy think about me when she's at work?" Maya asked.

"Always," said Dad. "She says you're her little spark of courage. Thinking of you makes her brave, even on the toughest nights."

"But why does she have to work at night?"

"Because emergencies can happen anytime," Dad explained. "And Mommy wants to make sure people have someone to help them when they need it most."

"Will she come home soon?" Maya asked as she yawned.

"Yes, sweetheart," Dad said, pulling the blanket snug around her. "And when she does, she'll be so happy to see you. She loves hearing about your dreams."

That night, Maya dreamed of her mom driving her firetruck under the stars, helping people stay safe. Even though she wasn't home, she knew she was a hero, and the stars were watching over both of them.

# Pictures of my Mom

# Pictures of me and my Mom

# Drawings of my Mom

# My favorite things about my Mom

Drawings of my mom at work

# Drawings of Mom and Dad

# Drawings of Dad tucking me in

# My favorite things about my Dad

www.ingramcontent.com/pod-product-compliance
Lightning Source LLC
Chambersburg PA
CBHW060539010526
44119CB00053B/765